SUPER SMOOTHIES
FOR NUTRIBULLET

SUPER SMOOTHIES
FOR NUTRIBULLET

More Than 75 Simple Recipes
to Supercharge Your Health

CHRISTINE KENT

Skyhorse Publishing

Recipes and images originally appeared in *Green Smoothie Joy* by Cressida Elias; *Green Smoothie Miracle* by Erica Palmcrantz Aziz; *Green Smoothies and Protein Drinks* by Jason Manheim; *Superfood Juices, Smoothies, and Drinks* by Jason Manheim; *Healthy Green Drink Diet* by Jason Manheim; *Healing Smoothies* by Daniella Chace; *Detox 101* by Jessi Andricks; *For the Love of Food and Yoga* by Live Yum LLC. For more information on these Skyhorse books and others, please see the back of this book.

Skyhorse Publishing books may be purchased in bulk at special discounts for sales promotion, corporate gifts, fund-raising, or educational purposes. Special editions can also be created to specifications. For details, contact the Special Sales Department, Skyhorse Publishing, 307 West 36th Street, 11th Floor, New York, NY 10018 or info@skyhorsepublishing.com.

Skyhorse® and Skyhorse Publishing® are registered trademarks of Skyhorse Publishing, Inc.®, a Delaware corporation.

Visit our website at www.skyhorsepublishing.com.

10 9 8 7 6 5 4 3 2

Library of Congress Cataloging-in-Publication Data is available on file.

Cover design by Eric Kang
Cover photo: Shutterstock

Print ISBN: 978-1-63450-849-0
Ebook ISBN: 978-1-63450-850-6

Printed in the United States of America

CONTENTS

INTRODUCTION

Like many people, I have often struggled to balance the demands of a busy work and home life with the need to keep happy and healthy. This tension became even more apparent to me when I became a wife and mother, roles which forced me to think even more carefully about food and the role it plays in my life. As my family grew, it became paramount to find quick, easy ways to prepare nutritious food that everyone could enjoy. On top of this, living in North Dakota, my family has always prided itself on living an active lifestyle with plenty of time spent in the outdoors, which means that our diet has to keep us energized and ready for whatever the day might bring. You don't want to run out of steam halfway through a hike or bike ride! However, initially, everything I tried seemed to require huge investments of time, money, and labor—all of which were in short supply in my busy household.

Then, one day, while I was dropping my daughter Sienna off for a playdate I saw her friend Megan drinking a curious and colorful beverage that caught my attention. I asked Megan's mother what it was, suspecting it was some new soda or "fruity beverage" loaded with sugar (and almost nothing else) that Sienna would be begging for soon. To my surprise, she informed me that the drink was a smoothie packed with veggies and fruits, and explained that their whole family had become addicted to them. When I got home, I got on my laptop and began to research smoothies and smoothie makers. The choices were seemingly endless; it seemed a movement had been building right under my nose. Despite the huge breadth of options, my goal was clear: to find a blender that was cheap, efficient, and easy to handle. We needed something that would fit easily into our hectic schedule but help us stay healthy. With these criteria set, the correct choice became clear pretty quickly: the NutriBullet.

"Why the NutriBullet," you ask? Simple. Unlike its competitors, the NutriBullet is designed to maximize both the nutrition of smoothies and the ease of making them. In contrast to traditional blenders, it uses a unique extraction system that pulls as many nutrients as possible out of the ingredients that you put into it. Moreover, with a simple and compact design, the NutriBullet can fit on any countertop and is easy to clean up after. All of these factors make it the perfect choice for anyone looking to incorporate smoothies into their regular diet, but especially for those who, like me, are on-the-go and need a hassle-free experience. I love that after I use it I can simply toss it into the dishwasher and come back a few hours later and it's ready to go again. Beyond this, it's been a source of great pleasure for my family to play with what we put into our NutriBullet and to tinker with recipes we've found online or that we've made ourselves. In fact, it was this creative nutritional collaboration that inspired me to put together this book.

I hope that *Super Smoothies for NutriBullet* can serve as a helpful primer for new and veteran NutriBullet users alike. When I first set out to make the book, I wanted to capture the sense of discovery and enjoyment that my own family had experienced in making our own smoothies. Hopefully, this book can help you expand what you eat and head further down the path of health and wellness. Good luck, and enjoy!

—Christine Kent

HEALING & REPLENISHING

HELLO WORLD

The perfect introduction to the language of green drinks. A quick look at the source code of this drink and you'll be surprised that its creamy blueberry goodness delivers such great flavor and nutrition. The energy surge will have you coding Hello World every morning.

1 CUP FRESH OR FROZEN ORGANIC BLUEBERRIES
2 BIG HANDFULS OF ORGANIC GREENS (WHATEVER YOU HAVE
    ON-HAND)
1 BANANA, PEELED
½ AVOCADO, PEELED AND PITTED

1 TEASPOON MATCHA
1 CUP WATER
1 ALMOND ICE
1 CUP ORGANIC RAW WHOLE MILK

Compile. Execute.

GREEN DETOX SMOOTHIE

1 CUP KALE
1 BANANA, PEELED
½ – 1 FRESHLY JUICED APPLE JUICE (OR
    PLAIN NON-DAIRY MILK)
JUICE OF 1 LEMON

Blend kale until chopped. Add in all other ingredients, adding in more liquid if needed, depending on the size of your fruit and speed of your blender.

BREAKFAST SMOOTHIE

Quality time for breakfast most mornings is non-existent. This smoothie is something good you can do for yourself that won't take much time, but will send you out into the world fortified with a tasty drink that will stick to your ribs.

1 BANANA, PEELED
½ CUP ORGANIC ROLLED OATS
2 TABLESPOONS HEMP SEEDS
1 TEASPOON MAQUI BERRY POWDER
1–2 CUPS WATER
1–2 CUPS ICE
CINNAMON AND SEA SALT TO TASTE

Blend all together in a high-powered blender.
Dust with cinnamon and serve.

PINEAPPLE & NECTARINE ENERGY SMOOTHIE

1 BANANA, PEELED
2 NECTARINES, PEELED AND PITTED
2 SLICES OF PINEAPPLE
1 CUP OF WATER OR MILK
1 TABLESPOON OF PROTEIN POWDER
    (VANILLA RICE PROTEIN)
WATER AND ICE AS NEEDED

Place all the ingredients into the NutriBullet and blend until smooth.

LIQUIDATE

You're going to hate when this one is gone. The dates do an awesome job of turning the bitterness of the dandelion greens into sweet bliss. You'll be purifying your liver and you won't even know it. There's a dose of healthy fats, too!

Replace the blueberries with raspberries and you'll have sweet, bitter, and sour all in one.

2 CUPS LAMB'S-QUARTERS OR DANDELION
    GREENS
3–4 DATES, PITTED
2 TABLESPOONS RAW ALMOND BUTTER
1 CUP COCONUT WATER
1 CUP FROZEN BLUEBERRIES

Add first 2 ingredients. Blend until smooth, adding water and coconut water as necessary. Add fruit and almond butter. Blend until desired consistency.

DAILY GREEN SMOOTHIE

Many of the green smoothies are based on what you have at home. Here is a variation on my "I'll-use-what-I-have-smoothie!"

2 CUPS MIXED SALAD
2 CUPS WATER
½ CUP BROCCOLI, CHOPPED
½ INCH CUCUMBER
1 KIWI, PEELED
2 PEARS, CORED AND PEELED
½ AVOCADO, PEELED AND PITTED

Mix the salad with the water. Add pieces of broccoli and cucumber. Blend. Add pieces of kiwi and pears. Scoop out the avocado and mix into the smoothie. Add more water until desired consistency is reached.

APPLE & CUCUMBER DETOX

2 APPLES, CORED AND PEELED
½ CUCUMBER, PEELED
1 AVOCADO, PEELED AND PITTED
A COUPLE OF SPRIGS OF PARSLEY
1 TEASPOON OF HONEY

Mix all in your NutriBullet and add some ice for coolness. Parsley has a strong taste, so you may have to add only a small amount according to taste.

AUTUMN BOOST

Rich pumpkin promotes healthy skin, and high fiber combined with açaí age-defying benefits make this team a pretty tasty pair. This harvest time multi-superfood concoction is like pumpkin pie for your skin!

½ CUP ORGANIC UNSWEETENED PUMPKIN
    PURÉE
½ OVERRIPE PEAR, CORED AND PEELED
2 TABLESPOONS AÇAÍ POWDER
2 TABLESPOONS FLAXSEED
2 TABLESPOONS DRIED MULBERRIES
1 CUP COCONUT WATER
1 CUP ICE

Blend all ingredients (except mulberries) together, sprinkle with mulberries, serve with a straw.

GORGEOUSLY GREEN SMOOTHIE

1 CUP KALE
1 CUP SPINACH
1 TO 2 FROZEN BANANAS, PEELED
½ – 1 CUP VANILLA COCONUT MILK
   (UNSWEETENED)

Add kale to the blender first and chop it up. Then add all other ingredients and blend until smooth. Pour into a cup and enjoy!

STRAWBERRY SAVASANA

The simple truth is that when we eat more fresh fruits and vegetables and fewer processed foods, we become healthier. Strawberries contain a plethora of very powerful antioxidants that help to counter the effects of free radicals. They also contain folic acid, which may aid in healthy pregnancies. The Strawberry Savasana smoothie is delicious and child-approved.

1 CUP FRESH STRAWBERRIES
1 CUP FROZEN STRAWBERRIES
½ CUP MANGO, DICED
1 FROZEN BANANA, PEELED

1 CUP STRAINED HONEY YOGURT
1 TABLESPOON AGAVE NECTAR
½ CUP COCONUT WATER
HIMALAYAN SALT COARSELY GROUND (TO TASTE)

Combine all ingredients in a blender. Serve.

MANGO CREAM

Bananas are rich in dopamine, which means they can enhance our mood while the dopamine's antioxidant properties provide protection from cancer development.

This tropical blend has a smooth and creamy texture and subtle mango fragrance.

½ BANANA, PEELED
½ CUP CARROT JUICE
½ CUP FROZEN MANGO, DICED
½ CUP FROZEN GREEN TEA CUBES
2 TABLESPOONS HULLED HEMP SEED
1 TEASPOON PROBIOTIC POWDER

Combine all ingredients and blend until smooth. Drink immediately.

QUICK COLD FIX

JUICE OF 1 ORANGE
A HANDFUL OF RASPBERRIES
1 KIWI, PEELED
A SQUEEZE OF LEMON
1 TEASPOON OF GREEN BARLEY GRASS OR
    OTHER GREEN SUPERFOOD
1 BANANA, PEELED
1 TEASPOON OF HONEY

Juice the orange. Combine in blender with other ingredients.

GREEN JAVA

Some of us can't even function until we get our morning coffee. A quick jolt of caffeine and energy is all you need, but what you tend to get is high calories, excess sugar, and a tainted smile. Hardly appealing when you can get twice the energy boost with none of those downfalls in a glass of wheatgrass-heavy Green Java.

Blend juiced wheatgrass with orange and banana to cut the bite of wheatgrass's intense flavor and pump you full of vitamin C and potassium.

1 BUNCH WHEATGRASS
2 ORANGES, PEELED
1 BANANA (OPTIONAL)
WATER/ICE

Fill NutriBullet with as much water/ice as you like, adding wheatgrass. Blend until smooth. Add fruit. Pulse-blend until desired consistency.

HEMP-POWERED PROTEIN

Not your average protein drink, this sinful solution provides the tastiest recovery from a workout you've had that doesn't involve a cheat day. Fruity chocolate raspberry flavor blended with creamy coconut milk and yogurt with a savory hint of turmeric inspires you to skip that cheat day and keep reaching for your goal.

2 TABLESPOONS HEMP SEED
1½ TABLESPOONS CACAO NIBS
1½ CUP FROZEN RASPBERRIES
½ CUP WHOLE MILK YOGURT

¼ TEASPOON TURMERIC
1 TABLESPOON CHOCOLATE PROTEIN POWDER
1 CUP COCONUT WATER

Place all ingredients in the NutriBullet and blend until smooth.

PERFECT POST-WORKOUT

After a serious workout where you've depleted your energy stores, it's important that you refuel your body to recover and get stronger so that you can meet your next personal record. Combining healthy carbs like rolled oats or organic rice with protein powder and natural sugar from raisins provides the substance you need to avoid muscle depletion and backsliding from your fitness progress.

1 CUP COOKED ORGANIC BROWN RICE (COLD) OR ½ CUP
    UNCOOKED ORGANIC ROLLED OATS
3–4 TABLESPOONS ORGANIC RAISINS
1–2 SCOOPS OF HIGH-QUALITY PROTEIN POWDER

1 TEASPOON CINNAMON
2 TEASPOON MACA POWDER
1 CUP WATER
1 CUP ORGANIC RAW WHOLE MILK

Combine all ingredients in your NutriBullet and blend until creamy.

POST-MARATHON

One of the integral parts of post-workout recovery is replacing lost fluids, and what better way to do that than with a superfood drink? Post Marathon's banana, citrus, and coconut combo meet these needs and are great for electrolyte replenishment. Starting a recovery routine is the best way to enhance overall workout performance and, with this drink, you are well on your way.

1 BANANA, PEELED
1 LEMON, PEELED
1 CUP COCONUT WATER
1½ CUPS ICE
1 CUP WATER

Blend all ingredients until smooth. Add protein or superfood powder, if necessary, and stir.

IRON SMOOTHIE

Parsley contains lots of iron, which is especially good for women.

2 CUPS FLAT-LEAF PARSLEY
2 CUPS WATER
2 APPLES, CORED AND PEELED
1 ZUCCHINI, PEELED
1 TABLESPOON LEMON JUICE

Mix parsley with water. Cut apples and zucchini into pieces. Add remaining ingredients and blend again. Dilute with more water until desired consistency is reached.

BLUE HIPPIE

Far out, man! Get the intense health boost of antioxidants in blueberries with the added benefits of hemp and flax seeds made creamy with almond milk. This drink will definitely make you one with the earthy flavors as well as help you feel totally groovy.

2 CUPS FRESH OR FROZEN ORGANIC
    BLUEBERRIES
1 TABLESPOON CHIA SEEDS (POWDER)
1 TABLESPOON FLAXSEED (POWDER)
1 TABLESPOON HEMP SEED (POWDER)
1 TABLESPOON COCONUT OIL
2 CUPS ALMOND MILK

Place all ingredients into one blender and blend until smooth.

BLUEBERRY BEET BAKASANA

Smoothies and juices provide a healthful, satisfying way to consume a variety of raw fruits and vegetables. Blueberries are repeatedly touted for having one of the highest antioxidant capacities. They also offer potential benefits for the nervous system and brain health. The Blueberry Beet Bakasana is a delicious, nutritious, vibrant-colored juice.

1 CUP BLUEBERRIES
1 LARGE BEET, PEELED
½ APPLE, CORED AND PEELED
1 KIWI, PEELED
2 STALKS OF CELERY
2 TABLESPOONS COCONUT WATER

Combine all ingredients in a blender. Serve.

BEAUTY BERRY

This drink couldn't be better for you if you wore it on your face. This one can make you beautiful on the inside as well as the outside.

1 RIPE AVOCADO, PEELED AND PITTED
1 TABLESPOON SOAKED GOJI BERRIES
1 TABLESPOON RAW HONEY
½ CUP WHOLE MILK YOGURT
½ SMALL CUCUMBER, JUICED
1 CUP COCONUT WATER

Blend all ingredients together and serve with a straw.

Change it up: Reduce coconut water to ½ cup and blend to make a delectable face mask that combats dry skin. Apply with fingers, careful not to get too close to your eyes. This is a wet mask, so leave it on for about 25 minutes before rinsing off with warm water.

BLACK CURRANT AND WILD BLUEBERRY

Blueberries are rich in phenolic compounds, which are high in antioxidants and thus inhibit the production of pro-inflammatory molecules, reduce oxidative stress, lessen DNA damage, and thwart cancer cell proliferation overall.

This smoothie has sweet wild blueberry and rich currant berry color and flavor.

½ CUP FROZEN WILD BLUEBERRIES
½ CUP BLACK CURRANT JUICE
½ CUP FROZEN GREEN TEA CUBES
2 TABLESPOONS PROTEIN POWDER

Combine all ingredients and blend until smooth.
Drink immediately.

APRICOT & MELON SMOOTHIE

This is a real summer smoothie with melon and fresh orange apricots. It's spiked with the power of sunflower shoots and spinach, and it's also hydrating because of the cucumber and water. Bring it in a thermos to the beach!

2 CUPS MELON, DICED
4 INCHES CUCUMBER, PEELED
1 CUP APRICOT, PITTED
1 CUP SPINACH
1 CUP SUNFLOWER SHOOTS
2 CUPS WATER

Cut the melon, cucumber, and apricots into chunks.
Mix with spinach, sunflower shoots, and water.
Dilute with water until desired consistency is reached.

ANTI-TOXI-MINT

Perfect for you trend dieters out there looking for better skin, antiaging properties, cancer fighters, and improving cognitive brain function. Truth be told, all greens can deliver these same benefits, but that's just not what the beauty magazines are about these days.

Even still, you can't beat the tart and tangy taste the Anti-toxi-mint delivers while still being the tabloid starlet who can do anything and everything (even help prevent cancer) and taste good doing it.

4–5 MINT LEAVES
½ ENGLISH CUCUMBER, PEELED
2 LARGE LEAVES COLLARD GREENS
½ CUP FROZEN AÇAÍ BERRIES
1 KIWI, PEELED
1 LEMON, JUICED

ADD FIRST 3 INGREDIENTS. BLEND UNTIL SMOOTH. ADD FRUIT. PULSE-BLEND UNTIL DESIRED CONSISTENCY.

GREEN AND CLEAN SMOOTHIE

1 CUP SPINACH
1 CUCUMBER, PEELED
1 APPLE, PEELED, CORED, AND CHOPPED
½ AVOCADO, PEELED AND PITTED
½–1 CUP WATER
JUICE OF 1 LEMON

Blend spinach in your blender to chop it up. Add in other ingredients except lemon. Squeeze lemon juice into the smoothie and blend again until smooth.

SWEET TREATS

Chocolate Chai	29
Monkeying Around	29
American Pie	31
Key Lime Split	31
Cherry Berry	33
Divine Dark Chocolate Gingerbread Cake	33
Paleo Chocolate Chip Smoothie	35
Creamy Walnut	35
Tart Apple Pom	37
Blood Orange Julius	37
Banana Bliss	39
Creamy Peanut Butter Berry Smoothie	39
Chocolate Mint	41
Banana Coconut Cocoa Cream	41
Cocoa Orange	43
Sweet Potato Pie	43
Banana Split	45
Blueberry Muffin	45
Vanilla Berry Lime	47

CHOCOLATE CHAI

Give in to the wonderful flavors of chocolate and banana melding together with a creamy chai tea. This combination is even more enjoyable when you know it is packing potassium and antioxidants in the same glass.

2 TABLESPOONS FLAX SEED
1 CUP CHAI TEA
½ CUP ORGANIC RAW WHOLE MILK
1 FROZEN BANANA, PEELED
2 TABLESPOONS CACAO NIBS
1 CUP ICE

Blend all ingredients together in your NutriBullet.

MONKEYING AROUND

Set the child in you free with the Monkeying Around shake. Enjoy the freedom of being! Almonds are a great source of protein and fiber.

1½ CUPS ALMOND MILK
3 BANANAS, PEELED
½ TEASPOONS GROUND CINNAMON
½ CUP OF ALMOND BUTTER
1 TABLESPOON AGAVE NECTAR
HIMALAYAN SALT COARSELY GROUND (TO
    TASTE)

Combine all ingredients in a blender. Serve.

AMERICAN PIE

Dessert in a glass. I recommend green-weary kids give this one a go before jumping in to something less sweet. Fresh young coconut is one of the most delicious healthy fats available. Mixed with sweet apples and protein-rich spinach, this is the closest you'll get to eating something akin to Grandma's pie without passing out after eating.

The banana is not optional in this one; it increases the potassium content of the spinach and adds a creamy pie-like texture that'll have you coming back for more.

2 GREEN APPLES, CORED
2 CUPS SPINACH
1 CUP YOUNG COCONUT FLESH
1 BANANA, PEELED
1 CUP COCONUT WATER
CINNAMON AND NUTMEG TO TASTE

Add first 3 ingredients. Blend until smooth, adding water as necessary. Add fruit and blend until desired consistency.

KEY LIME SPLIT

This Key Lime Split smoothie is totally refreshing. Nutrient-dense coconut combined with fresh fruits and zesty key limes create a well-balanced drink. Key limes are full of one of nature's best antioxidants, Vitamin C.

2 TABLESPOONS COCONUT SOLIDS FROM REFRIGERATED (OVERNIGHT) UNSHAKEN CAN OF COCONUT MILK (LIQUID POURED OFF)
1 TABLESPOON COCONUT WATER
2 TABLESPOONS AGAVE NECTAR

½ FROZEN, PEELED BANANA
½ CUP FRESH PINEAPPLE
JUICE FROM TWO KEY LIMES (REGULAR LIMES MAY BE SUBSTITUTED)
1 CUP ICE

Combine all ingredients in a blender. Serve.

CHERRY BERRY

2 CUPS OF CHERRIES (PITTED)
1 BANANA, PEELED
1 CUP OF RASPBERRIES
1 APPLE, CORED
DARK CHOCOLATE CHUNKS OR 1–2 TSP OF
    COCOA POWDER OR CACAO
NIBS (OPTIONAL)
1 CUP OF WATER
ICE

Blend all the ingredients along with the ice and a little water. Add more water if you need it.

DIVINE DARK CHOCOLATE GINGERBREAD CAKE

Yum, yum, yum! This beverage would make a wake-up-worthy breakfast treat.

2 tablespoons coconut solids from refrigerated (overnight) unshaken can of coconut milk (liquid poured off)

½ CUP ALMOND MILK
1 FROZEN BANANA, PEELED
1 TABLESPOON DARK COCOA POWDER
1 TEASPOON GROUND GINGER

½ CUP OF ALMOND BUTTER
3 TABLESPOONS PURE MAPLE SYRUP
HIMALAYAN SALT COARSELY GROUND (TO TASTE)

Combine all ingredients in a blender. Serve.

PALEO CHOCOLATE CHIP SMOOTHIE

½ CUP SOAKED ALMONDS
½ CUP COCONUT MILK
½ CUP COCONUT WATER
2 TABLESPOONS CACAO NIBS
1 VANILLA BEAN OR 1 TEASPOON EXTRACT
1–2 TEASPOON PURE MAPLE SYRUP
    (OPTIONAL)
½ TEASPOON SEA SALT
2 CUPS ICE

Skip the cookie sheet! Skin almonds and place in your NutriBullet with all other delicious ingredients. Blend until it resembles chocolate chip ice cream. Serve with a straw and enjoy the cacao crunch!

CREAMY WALNUT

The rich, natural flavor of walnuts combined with dates and yogurt bring out the nutty goodness of this drink. Flax seed delivers a fiber boost that is healthy and satisfying any time of the day.

1 TABLESPOON FLAX SEED
¼ CUP SOAKED WALNUTS
2–3 DATES, PITTED
½ CUP ORGANIC WHOLE MILK YOGURT
½ CUP FRESH YOUNG COCONUT WATER
1–2 CUPS ICE
STEVIA TO TASTE (OPTIONAL)

Blend all ingredients together and enjoy!

TART APPLE POM

The skin of apples contains exceptionally high concentrations of antioxidants that have been found to reduce the growth of cancer cells.

This sweet apple and grape smoothie is creamy with a little tartness from the grapefruit.

½ CUP GRAPEFRUIT, PEELED
½ CUP APPLE, CORED
½ CUP FROZEN RED GRAPES
½ CUP POMEGRANATE JUICE
2 TABLESPOONS CHIA SEED

Combine all ingredients and blend until smooth.
Drink immediately.

BLOOD ORANGE JULIUS

Pretty in pink, this creamy dreamsicle smoothie will absolutely surprise you. Its sinful flavor conceals its healthful nature. With every sip, you'd never guess you were taking in healthy probiotics, fighting disease, and reducing inflammation.

1 BLOOD ORANGE, PEELED
1 CUP ORGANIC WHOLE MILK YOGURT
½ CUP DRIED MULBERRIES
1 VANILLA BEAN OR ½ TEASPOON EXTRACT
1 TEASPOON HONEY
½ CUP COCONUT WATER
1½ CUPS ICE

Juice blood orange and set aside. Blend all other ingredients together. Once blended, pulse to mix in the orange juice.

BANANA BLISS

If there's such a thing as bliss-in-a-cup, this is it! Plus, bananas contain potassium, which reduces swelling, increases energy, strengthens our nervous system, and improves digestion.

1 CUP CHOPPED TOASTED NUTS (WALNUTS, PECANS, OR COMBINATION)
2 TABLESPOONS BROWN SUGAR
3 FROZEN BANANAS, PEELED

2 TABLESPOONS ALMOND MILK
1 16 OZ. REFRIGERATED (OVERNIGHT) UNSHAKEN CAN OF COCONUT MILK (LIQUID POURED OFF)
1 TEASPOON VANILLA EXTRACT

Toast nuts in a medium skillet over low-medium heat, adding salt to taste throughout the process, until golden brown and fragrant. Stir in brown sugar and cook for another 1 to 2 minutes, or until sugar is dissolved. Remove from heat and place in refrigerator.

Combine bananas, almond milk, coconut solids, and vanilla in food processor until just combined. Add cool nuts and pulse slightly.

Serve immediately in individual glasses. Enjoy!

CREAMY PEANUT BUTTER BERRY SMOOTHIE

1 BANANA, PEELED
1 CUP OF MIXED FROZEN BERRIES
½ CUP OF CREAM
2 CUPS OF WATER
1 TABLESPOON OF PEANUT BUTTER (UNSWEETENED)
1 TEASPOON OF COCOA POWDER OR CACAO POWDER
2 TEASPOONS MAPLE SYRUP OR AGAVE SYRUP

Put the banana and strawberry chunks into the NutriBullet. Pour in the water and cream, then the rest of the ingredients. Blend until smooth.

CHOCOLATE MINT

Chocolate and mint together provide a tasty treat that never fails to satisfy. Reminiscent of cookie and candy standards, Chocolate Mint pays homage to some nostalgic favorites. With this creamy drink, you can enjoy the combination guilt-free with the added bonus that it is actually good for you!

4 DATES, PITTED
1–2 CUPS RAW MILK (OR ALMOND MILK)
¼ CUP SOAKED ALMONDS
2 TABLESPOONS CACAO NIBS
½ CUP PACKED MINT LEAVES
½ SMALL AVOCADO, PEELED AND PITTED
2 CUPS COCONUT ICE

Skin all soaked almonds before placing them and the rest of the ingredients in the NutriBullet to blend to a chunky minty goodness.

BANANA COCONUT COCOA CREAM

Cocoa is an excellent source of the mineral magnesium, which helps reduce inflammation and free radicals thus providing some protection against oxidative DNA damage that can lead to cancer development.

This creamy, comforting whip has distinctive cocoa, banana, and coconut flavors.

1 BANANA, PEELED
1 CUP CULTURED COCONUT MILK
½ CUP FROZEN WHITE TEA CUBES
2 TABLESPOONS UNSWEETENED COCOA
    POWDER
2 TABLESPOONS PROTEIN POWDER

COCOA ORANGE

Cryptoxanthin, a provitamin carotenoid in mandarin oranges, has proven to be effective at suppressing the growth and spread of stomach cancer cells in laboratory studies.

Fragrant with rich chocolate and orange scent, this smoothie is not too sweet and layered with rich flavors.

1 MANDARIN ORANGE, PEELED
1 FROZEN BANANA, PEELED
½ CUP ORANGE JUICE
½ CUP CULTURED COCONUT MILK
½ CUP FROZEN GREEN TEA CUBES
2 TABLESPOONS PROTEIN POWDER
2 TABLESPOONS UNSWEETENED COCOA
     POWDER

Combine all ingredients and blend until smooth. Drink immediately.

SWEET POTATO PIE

Even if autumn is not quite yet in the air, you can bring the nostalgia and flavors of the season into your morning smoothies or have it as dessert. Sweet potatoes are a nutritional superstar that are high in dietary fibers, beta-carotene, and complex carbohydrates and are known to improve blood sugar regulation and digestion.

Fennel, while adding a warm licorice flavor, is also good for digestive health and often used to combat bad breath. Ground flaxseed is rich in omega-3 fatty acids, high in fiber, and adds a nutty element, all together giving you a tasty, low-starch, guilt-free take on a classic seasonal dessert.

1 CUP SEMI-COOKED SWEET POTATO (OR ½
     JUICED)
1 TABLESPOON GROUND FLAX
½ FENNEL/ANISE BULB
1 ORANGE, PEELED
2 CUPS SPINACH
1–2 FRESH FIGS
1 CUP COCONUT WATER
CINNAMON TO TASTE

Add all ingredients. Blend until smooth, adding water as necessary.

BANANA SPLIT

Resveratrol, found in peanuts and peanut butter, has been found to suppress intestinal cancers.

The cocoa and vanilla fragrances stimulate the appetite while the peanut butter and vanilla bean flavor hit the palate. The taste is reminiscent of slightly melted chocolate ice cream.

1 FROZEN BANANA, PEELED
1 VANILLA BEAN
1 CUP ALMOND MILK
½ CUP FROZEN CHERRIES, PITTED
2 TABLESPOONS PEANUT BUTTER
2 TABLESPOONS VANILLA PROTEIN POWDER
2 TABLESPOONS HULLED HEMP SEED
2 TABLESPOONS UNSWEETENED COCOA
    POWDER

Combine all ingredients and blend until smooth. Drink immediately.

BLUEBERRY MUFFIN

1 CUP FRESH/FROZEN BLUEBERRIES
½ CUP CANNED PUMPKIN
2 FIGS
1 BANANA, PEELED
2–3 LARGE KALE LEAVES, STEMMED
1 TABLESPOON CHIA SEEDS
1 CUP COCONUT WATER

Blend until smooth. Adjust liquid/ice as necessary.

VANILLA BERRY LIME

Vanilla contains vanillin, which directly reduces cancer growth and development.

This citrus and berry smoothie is sweet and tart and tastes a bit like candy but less sweet as it is tempered by the tea and hemp protein.

1 LIME WEDGE, PEELED
1 VANILLA BEAN
½ CUP TANGERINE
½ CUP POMEGRANATE JUICE
½ CUP FROZEN STRAWBERRIES
½ CUP CULTURED COCONUT MILK
½ CUP FROZEN GREEN TEA CUBES
2 TABLESPOONS HULLED HEMP SEED

Combine all ingredients and blend until smooth.
Drink immediately.

COCKTAIL-INSPIRED

BIRD OF PARADISE PIÑA COLADA

As we find when moving into Bird of Paradise pose, the beauty lies at the fine line between effort and ease. Here we are comfortable with our actions and inactions. Here we blossom! The Bird of Paradise Piña Colada smoothie contains coconut solids and coconut water. Many Asian and Pacific populations call the coconut palm "The Tree of Life," as they consider it to be the cure for illness as well as a great food source; it is rich in fiber, vitamins, and minerals.

2 TABLESPOONS COCONUT SOLIDS FROM
 REFRIGERATED (OVERNIGHT) UNSHAKEN
 CAN OF COCONUT MILK (LIQUID POURED
 OFF)
1 CUP COCONUT WATER
½ FROZEN BANANA, PEELED
1 CUP FRESH MANGO, PEELED AND DICED
1 ½ CUPS FRESH PINEAPPLE, DICED
½ CUP ICE
AGAVE NECTAR TO TASTE (OPTIONAL)

Combine all ingredients in a blender. Serve.

TROPICAL SUN

You may not be able to make it to the tropics before breakfast, but you can sure make it to the blender to make yourself this delicious flavor getaway.

Before your daily grind starts, treat yourself to the rich vitamins orange and pineapple have to offer. Bok choy, categorized as a negative-calorie food by its ability to facilitate the burning of calories, tastes amazing alongside its tropical components. Throw in a tiny umbrella for good measure and you won't be missing any nutrients; all you'll be missing is the beach.

2 BULBS BOK CHOY
1 ORANGE, PEELED
1 CUP COCONUT WATER
1 CUP PINEAPPLE, DICED
1 BANANA, PEELED

Add first 3 ingredients. Blend until smooth. Add fruit. Pulse-blend until desired consistency.

BLOODY MERRY (A.K.A. HAIR OF THE DOG)

This is perfect for when you're feeling under the weather, dehydrated, or just want a rejuvenating drink. Horseradish is included because it adds a great kick and also contains cancer-fighting compounds called glucosinolates.

4 LARGE TOMATOES, SEEDED
2 STALKS CELERY (LEAVES REMOVED)
1 TABLESPOON FRESH GINGER
1 MEDIUM GARLIC CLOVE
1 TABLESPOON FRESH HORSERADISH
2 TABLESPOONS LEMON JUICE

1 TEASPOON LEMON FLAXSEED OIL
1 TEASPOON TAMARI
DASH OF CAYENNE
DASH OF TURMERIC
DASH OF CELERY SALT
PEPPER COARSELY GROUND (TO TASTE)

Combine ingredients in a blender. Serve.

CURRANT GRAPE TEA

Berries provide quercetin, which is a flavonoid known for its ability to reduce the severity of allergic reactions and reduce cancer-induced inflammation. This intense, fruity combination has a light tea and citrus fragrance.

1 LIME WEDGE, PEELED
½ CUP CURRANT JUICE
½ CUP FROZEN GRAPES
½ CUP WATERMELON, DICED
½ CUP FROZEN GREEN TEA CUBES
2 TABLESPOONS CHIA SEED

Combine all ingredients and blend until smooth.
Drink immediately.

SWEET HOT MARGARITA

2 CUPS WATERMELON, DICED
1 LEMON, PEELED
1 LARGE HANDFUL ARUGULA
¼ JALAPEÑO (OR TO TASTE)
DASH OF CAYENNE
1 TEASPOON AGAVE NECTAR (OR TO TASTE)
2 CUPS ICE

Blend until smooth. Add more water or ice if necessary. Pour into chili-powder-rimmed glass with ice cubes.

CRAZY CRAN

This is not your regular cranberry cocktail, no, sir. This veritable dynamo of vitamins has it all. A high source of fiber in both mixed baby greens and collard greens with mint offering healthful digestive properties and cranberries providing bacteria blockers.

No jug of juice offers even a fraction of what Crazy Cran brings to the breakfast table. So blend up a glass and toast to your health.

1 CUP FROZEN CRANBERRIES
1 ORANGE, PEELED
2 LEAVES COLLARD GREENS
1 BUNCH MIXED BABY GREENS
3–4 MINT LEAVES
1 PEAR, CORED
1 CUP COCONUT WATER
1 LEMON, JUICED
1 BANANA (OPTIONAL)

Add first 4 ingredients. Blend until smooth, adding water, lemon juice, and coconut water as necessary. Add fruit. Pulse-blend until desired consistency.

HABANERO AND CITRUS

Tangeretin is a naturally occurring plant compound found in significant amounts in the peel of citrus fruits. Tangeretin dramatically reduced breast cancer cells in lab studies and repeated studies have found that tangeretin is effective at causing apoptosis in many types of cancer.

Ice-cold and spicy hot, this combination has a hot pepper bite and a light citrus note with sweet berry and bitter orange.

¼ ORANGE, PEELED
¼ SMALL HABANERO PEPPER, SEEDED
½ CUP WATERMELON, DICED
½ CUP FROZEN GREEN TEA CUBES
½ CUP FROZEN STRAWBERRIES
2 TABLESPOONS HULLED HEMP SEED

Combine all ingredients and blend until smooth.
Drink immediately.

MANGO MINT-JITO

For the lush in all of us. Except, you know . . . without all the stumbling and liver damage. In fact, with the amount of fiber and enzymes in mangoes, you can lower LDL cholesterol and improve digestion. A fresher, healthier approach to its boozier counterpart, the Mango Mint-jito's sweet tropical flavors will leave you hungry for a day by the pool instead of a night hugging the toilet.

1 CUP MANGO, PEELED AND DICED
2 CUPS LETTUCE GREENS
5 LARGE MINT LEAVES
½ LEMON, JUICED
½ LIME, JUICED
1 BANANA (OPTIONAL)
WATER/ICE

Fill blender with as much water/ice as you like,
adding mint and greens. Blend until smooth.
Add fruit. Pulse-blend until desired consistency.

Cocktail-inspired

STRAWBERRY AND BASIL LEMONADE

Basil contains powerful antioxidants that protect against cellular damage and provide proven protection against breast cancer development.

This light smoothie has a fresh basil fragrance and sweet strawberry flavor with a citrus finish.

½ CUP STRAWBERRIES
½ CUP FRESH BASIL LEAVES
½ CUP WATER
½ CUP FROZEN GREEN TEA CUBES
2 TABLESPOONS CHIA SEED
1 TABLESPOON LEMON JUICE

Combine all ingredients and blend until smooth.
Drink immediately.

WATERMELON BLACKBERRY CITRUS

Berries and berry juices contain active compounds that counteract, reduce, and repair damage to cells resulting from oxidative stress and inflammation. The sweetness of the berries and the watermelon in this blend are balanced by the bitterness of the rosemary and the acidity of the lime. The bitter compounds in the rosemary support digestion and help stimulate the release of digestive enzymes and hydrochloric acid.

½ CUP WATERMELON, DICED
½ CUP COCONUT WATER
½ CUP FROZEN BLACKBERRIES
½ CUP FROZEN GREEN TEA CUBES
2 TABLESPOONS LIME JUICE
2 TABLESPOONS HULLED HEMP SEED
1 TABLESPOON FRESH ROSEMARY

Combine all ingredients and blend until smooth.
Drink immediately.

Cocktail-inspired

WATERMELON BLACKBERRY AND GINGER

Ginger contains gingerol, which is the major pungent component of ginger. Gingerol reduces cancer growth by inhibiting the metastatic process.

This smoothie has fresh watermelon and blackberry flavor with a little bit of heat from the ginger.

½ CUP ORANGE JUICE
½ CUP WATERMELON, DICED
½ CUP FROZEN BLACKBERRIES
½ CUP FROZEN PINEAPPLE, DICED
½ CUP FROZEN GREEN TEA CUBES
2 TABLESPOONS HULLED HEMP SEED
1 TABLESPOON FRESH GINGER ROOT

Combine all ingredients and blend until smooth. Drink immediately.

SANGRIA BLANCA

1–2 WHITE PEACHES, PITTED
1 CUP RAINIER CHERRIES, PITTED
1–2 WHITE NECTARINES, PITTED
1 CUP GREEN GRAPES
6–10 ENDIVE LEAVES
3–5 MINT LEAVES

Blend with water and ice to desired consistency.

FUN & FRUITY

RED RASPBERRY SMOOTHIE

1 CUP COCONUT MILK OR COCONUT WATER
1 CUP FRESH RASPBERRIES
1 FROZEN BANANA, PEELED
2 TABLESPOONS CHIA SEEDS

Add all ingredients to your NutriBullet; turn it on and blend until smooth.

CREAMY APRICOT SMOOTHIE

Dried apricots should be brown. Avoid buying the orange ones, which are sulfurized, meaning that sulfur has been added. This is done to inhibit bacteria and fungi and to preserve the color. However, this can also cause asthma.

1 CUP NETTLE
1 CUP SPINACH
½ CUP OF SOAKING WATER
1 ½ CUP WATER
1 RED APPLE, CORED
8 SOAKED APRICOTS, SOAKED 2–4 HOURS

Chop the nettles and mix with spinach, water, and the water from the apricots. Add pieces of apples and apricots, and blend again.

GUAVACADO

Guavas can be hard to come by and vary quite drastically in size, shape, and texture. Test the seeds before you toss this one into the NutriBullet as some can be as hard as stones.

Also, some guava skin can be thick and bitter, so be sure to test that too. All this work just for a smoothie? You won't be disappointed once that creamy avocado texture hits your lips.

1 CUP GUAVA
1 AVOCADO, PEELED AND PITTED
2 CUPS RED LEAF LETTUCE
1 CUP MANGO, PEELED AND DICED
1 LEMON, JUICED
1 CUP COCONUT WATER

Add all ingredients. Blend until smooth, adding water as necessary.

COCO MANGO SMOOTHIE

Great for a quick fruit blast.

1 MANGO, PEELED
1 BANANA, PEELED
2 SLICES OF PINEAPPLE, JUICED
1 TABLESPOON OF COCONUT CREAM OR 1
    CUP OF COCONUT MILK
WATER
ICE

Just put the ingredients into the NutriBullet and whizz it!

MELON BERRY CITRUS

Naringenin is a flavonoid, found in grapefruit and oranges, that acts as an antioxidant to provide protection from genetic mutations that can lead to cancer. This blend is cool, lush and slightly tart with rich fruit flavor.

½ CUP GRAPEFRUIT, PEELED
½ CUP WATERMELON, DICED
½ CUP FROZEN RED RASPBERRIES
½ CUP POMEGRANATE JUICE
½ CUP FROZEN GREEN TEA CUBES
2 TABLESPOONS CHIA SEED

Combine all ingredients and blend until smooth. Drink immediately.

FRUIT COCKTAIL

2 CUPS WATERMELON, CHOPPED
1 CUP STRAWBERRIES
1 CUP GRAPES
3–5 LEAVES OF MINT
1 LARGE HANDFUL MIXED GREENS

Blend with ice. Add more watermelon for desired consistency.

SWEET MINT

Optional Protein: Chia seeds

1–2 LARGE COLLARD LEAVES
1 PEAR, CORED
1 KIWI, PEELED
1 CUP BLACKBERRIES
1 CUP BLUEBERRIES
3–6 MINT LEAVES

Blend with water and ice to desired consistency.

BLUEBERRY MAGIC SMOOTHIE

The base is green, but you would never know. It's like magic! Makes 2 servings

1 CUP FROZEN BLUEBERRIES AND/OR
    BLACKBERRIES
2 FROZEN BANANAS, PEELED
1 CUP UNSWEETENED ALMOND MILK
2–3 HANDFULS OF SPINACH
½ CUCUMBER, PEELED

*OPTIONAL NATURAL LIQUID SWEETENER
    TO TASTE

Blend all ingredients until smooth.

APPLE RAZ

The sweetness of the red apple and the sour tang of the fresh raspberries and lemon balance out the bold flavor of the calcium-rich kale. Baby greens add a boost of vitamins and really makes this a well-rounded green drink.

A great way to kick off your morning!

1 RED APPLE, CORED
1 CUP FRESH RASPBERRIES
⅛ HONEYDEW MELON, DICED
1 BIG KALE LEAF (REMOVE STEM)
1 HANDFUL BABY GREENS
1 LEMON, JUICED
1 BANANA (OPTIONAL), PEELED
WATER/ICE

Fill blender with water/ice, add kale, greens, and apple. Blend until smooth. Add remaining ingredients. Pulse-blend until desired consistency.

POMEGRANATE GREEN SMOOTHIE

1 CUP BLUEBERRIES
A FEW DRIED GOJI BERRIES
½ CUP FRESH POMEGRANATE JUICE
    (JUICE FROM APPROXIMATELY 2
    POMEGRANATES)
1 BANANA, PEELED
2 HANDFULS OF LAMB'S LETTUCE
2 CUPS OF WATER
SOME ICE

Juice the pomegranates. Blend with the other ingredients.

BLACKBERRY BLUE-GREEN SMOOTHIE

2 HANDFULS OF SWISS CHARD
1 CUP OF BLUEBERRIES
1 CUP OF BLACKBERRIES
1 FROZEN BANANA, PEELED
1 CUP OF WATER

Mix all ingredients in your NutriBullet until smooth.

STRAWBERRY PATCH

A sweet treat and an easy way to introduce dark greens like collards into your diet. Collards have a strong, distinct flavor especially when cooked, but when blended raw among earthy-sweet and tropical flavors like kiwi and strawberry, you'll find collards are great at adding a spicy zing to an otherwise typical fruit smoothie.

Mangoes add a list of health benefits to the smoothie with enzymes that aid healthy digestion, glutamine for memory power, and heart-healthy antioxidants.

3 STRAWBERRIES
1 MANGO, PEELED AND PITTED
1 KIWI, PEELED
3 BIG BASIL LEAVES
2 LARGE COLLARD LEAVES (REMOVE STEMS)
WATER

Fill blender with as much water as you like, adding collard greens and basil. Blend until smooth. Add fruit. Pulse-blend until desired consistency.

KIWI PARADISE GREEN SMOOTHIE

1 APPLE, CORED
2 KIWIS, PEELED
1 HANDFUL OF SWISS CHARD
½ AVOCADO, PEELED AND PITTED

A SQUEEZE OF LIME
2 MINT LEAVES (OPTIONAL)
1 CUP OF WATER
ICE

Juice the apple and add to the NutriBullet. Add all other ingredients and blend.

STRAW-MEGRANATE

Big, bold strawberry flavor with a tarty pomegranate kick. This antioxidant-rich smoothie may decrease the risk of heart disease and guard against free-radical damage. Blending pomegranate seeds can be tough for some blenders, so if you have trouble, try replacing them with some fresh-squeezed juice or a cup of store-bought pomegranate juice.

6 STRAWBERRIES
1 CUP POMEGRANATE SEEDS
1 RED APPLE, CORED
1 STALK CELERY
1 PEACH
1 HANDFUL RED GRAPES
2 HANDFULS FRESH SPINACH
1 BANANA (OPTIONAL)
WATER

Fill blender with as much water as you like.
And ingredients. Blend until smooth.

BLACK MELON

An easy way to start introducing greens into your smoothies is to start off sweet. This drink is higher in natural sugars but still provides essential nutrients without the added preservatives and refined sugars. Black Melon contains high amounts of antioxidants, fiber, and vitamin C.

Spinach, an amazing source of protein, has a very subtle flavor and is often completely masked by any sweetness from fruit. Taking care of your body has never tasted so good.

½ CUP WATERMELON, DICED
½ CUP HONEYDEW MELON, DICED
½ CUP CANTALOUPE, DICED
½ CUP BLACKBERRIES
2 HANDFULS FRESH SPINACH
1 BANANA (OPTIONAL)
WATER/ICE

Fill blender with as much water/ice as you like, adding greens. Blend until smooth. Add fruit. Pulse-blend until desired consistency.

PAPAYA STRAWBERRY SMOOTHIE

1 PAPAYA, PEELED AND DICED
½ FROZEN BANANA, PEELED
1 SLICE OF PINEAPPLE
1 HANDFUL OF STRAWBERRIES
1 CUP OF WATER
ICE

Blend all ingredients and then add the ice.

SWEET CITRUS CARROT

Bananas contain prebiotics including inulin and fructo-oligosaccharides that stimulate the growth of beneficial gut flora such as Bifidobacterium, which not only improves digestion but also provides protection from fungal and bacterial infections.

This tropical blend is fresh and light with subtle sweet carrot flavor.

2 MANDARIN ORANGES, PEELED
½ BANANA, PEELED
½ CUP PINEAPPLE, DICED
½ CUP CARROT JUICE
½ CUP FROZEN GREEN TEA CUBES
2 TABLESPOONS HULLED HEMP SEED

Combine all ingredients and blend until smooth.
Drink immediately.

JUST PEACHY

Here's a simple one. Great for kids and those having trouble incorporating greens into their diets. Spinach really packs a punch. It's a common green; you can get it just about anywhere, it's affordable, and the taste is mild enough that anyone can enjoy it. It's a great source of iron and beta-carotene and protects from a multitude of maladies. And who doesn't like peaches?

4 PEACHES, PITTED
1–2 CUPS SPINACH
WATER/ICE

Fill blender with as much water/ice as you like and add ingredients. Blend until smooth.

Fun & fruity

GRAPEFRUIT ROSEMARY

Nobiletin is one of the bioflavonoids found in citrus fruits such as lemons, oranges, tangerines, and grapefruits. Nobiletin has anti-inflammatory and anticancer actions and the potential to suppress metastasis of breast cancer.

This frosty blend has a perfect balance of citrus with a hint of bitterness from the grapefruit and rosemary. The flavor and fragrance are energizing, making this an excellent morning blend.

1 CUP GRAPEFRUIT, PEELED
½ CUP CHERRIES, PITTED
½ CUP ORANGE JUICE
½ CUP FROZEN GREEN TEA CUBES
2 TABLESPOONS HULLED HEMP SEED
1 TABLESPOON FRESH ROSEMARY

Combine all ingredients and blend until smooth.
Drink immediately.

VEGGIELICIOUS

FLYING CARROT

Carrots contain the antioxidant beta-carotene and are an excellent source of Vitamin A, helping us to glow from the inside out. The Flying Carrot combines a perfect combination of savory and sweet flavors.

2 CARROTS
¼ BANANA, PEELED
½ CUP SOY MILK
¼ CUP HONEY YOGURT
1 TABLESPOON FRESH GINGER

Combine all ingredients in a blender. Serve.

GINGER GREEN SMOOTHIE

2 HANDFULS OF KALE
2 CUPS WATER
6 SOAKED FIGS, 2–4 HOURS
½ INCH GINGER

Chop the kale and mix with 1 cup of water. Add figs and peeled, chopped ginger and blend again. Add water until desired consistency is reached.

PLUMKIN

Optional Protein: Whole milk plain yogurt

Add whole milk, chia seeds, or your favorite protein powder to make the perfect post-workout recovery green smoothie.

1–2 SPOONFULS PUMPKIN PURÉE
1–2 PLUMS, PITTED
1 LARGE HANDFUL SPINACH
CINNAMON TO TASTE
2 CUPS COCONUT WATER

Blend and add more coconut water as necessary.

POMEGREEN SMOOTHIE

Tip! To pick out the small red pomegranate seeds, cut the fruit in half, gently squeeze the skin, and turn it inside out over a bowl. Remove the seeds. Discard the white parts of the skin, which can taste bitter. Strain the juice, pour into a beautiful glass, and add the kernels to the smoothie.

2 CUPS SALAD
1–2 CUPS WATER
2 PEARS, CORED
1 CUP (ABOUT ½ POMEGRANATE)
    POMEGRANATE KERNELS.

Blend the salad with 1 cup of water. Cut the pear into pieces and add the other ingredients before mixing again. Add more water until desired consistency is reached.

COL. MUSTARD GREENS

Works well with fresh oregano, basil, or dill, but feel free to experiment with other fresh herbs.

2 CUPS MUSTARD GREENS
2–3 ROMA TOMATOES
¼ AVOCADO, PEELED AND PITTED
1 SMALL ZUCCHINI
1 LIME, PEELED
FAVORITE HERBS TO TASTE

Blend with water to desired consistency.

JUST BEET IT

Beets are essential for heart health and have an earthy-sweet taste. Arugula contains antiviral and antibacterial properties as well as high levels of vitamin K. Though it's known to have a bitter taste, when paired with an apple and banana, there's nothing bitter . . . or should I say, better.

1 MEDIUM BEET, PEELED AND DICED
2 CUPS ARUGULA
1 RED APPLE, CORED
4–5 BASIL LEAVES
1 BANANA, PEELED

APPLE SPROUTS

¼ OF A SMALL RED ONION
1 APPLE, CORED
1 PEAR, CORED
1 HANDFUL SPINACH
3–4 BRUSSELS SPROUTS
GINGER TO TASTE

Blend with water and ice to desired consistency.

THAI DANCER

When concentrating on maintaining deep and steady breathing in yoga as well as treating poses and transitions as postures, we begin to float or even dance throughout our practices. The Thai Dancer juice is inspired by Thai cooking flavors and packs a sweet and spicy punch. This makes a great mid-afternoon juice.

1 CUP KALE
¼ CUP CILANTRO LEAVES
1 TABLESPOON MINT LEAVES
¼ SERRANO CHILI PEPPER, SEEDED
½ CUP FRESH PINEAPPLE, DICED
2 TABLESPOONS LIME JUICE

Combine all ingredients in a blender. Serve chilled.

AVO-COOLER

1 BUNCH WATERCRESS
3–6 LARGE MINT LEAVES
1 LIME, PEELED OR JUICED
1 CUCUMBER, PEELED
½ AVOCADO, PEELED AND PITTED

Blend until smooth. Add ice or water to thin.

MANGOMOLE

1 MANGO, PEELED AND PITTED
1 PEACH, PITTED
1 HANDFUL SPINACH
1 SMALL BUNCH CILANTRO
¼ SMALL ONION
¼ AVOCADO, PEELED AND PITTED
½ YELLOW BELL PEPPER
JALAPEÑO TO TASTE
½ LEMON, PEELED

Blend with water and ice to desired consistency.

SOUP TO GOJI

A play on a savory summer soup favorite, Soup To Goji adds a sour, spicy element to the rustic Italian flavors of a classic gazpacho. Goji berries are great additions to many savory snacks.

2 ORGANIC ROMA TOMATOES
1 HANDFUL ORGANIC PARSLEY
1 HANDFUL ORGANIC CILANTRO
1 SMALL ORGANIC CUCUMBER, PEELED
1 CLOVE GARLIC
1–2 TABLESPOONS GOJI BERRIES
½ LEMON, JUICED
½ CUP WATER
2 TABLESPOONS EXTRA VIRGIN OLIVE OIL
SALT, PEPPER, AND CAYENNE TO TASTE

Place all ingredients, except the oil, into the NutriBullet. After initially blended, pulse while drizzling in the oil. Serve in bowl or large cappuccino mug with a spoon.

TROPICANA

1 HANDFUL ARUGULA
1 ORANGE, PEELED
½ YELLOW BELL PEPPER
1–2 CUPS PINEAPPLE, DICED
1 HANDFUL SPINACH

Blend with water and ice to desired consistency.

GAZPACHO

1–2 ROMA TOMATOES
½ RED BELL PEPPER
1 GARLIC CLOVE
¼ SMALL ONION
1 HANDFUL CILANTRO
1 HANDFUL PARSLEY
JALAPEÑO TO TASTE
TARRAGON TO TASTE

Blend with water and ice to desired consistency.

WASABI SMOOTHIE

You normally eat wasabi with sushi, but in this case, it adds a little extra heat to the smoothie. If you don't have wasabi paste, use wasabi powder and adjust the amount according to taste.

4 CELERY STALKS
1 CUCUMBER, PEELED
1/5 CUP WATER
1/10 INCH WASABI PASTE
2 TABLESPOONS HONEY

Chop celery and cucumber into pieces. Blend with the water. Add remaining ingredients and mix again.

GREEN X3 SMOOTHIE

Green from green leaves, green from the algae spirulina, and green from wheat grass powder—it doesn't get any better than this.

1 CUP SPINACH
2 CUPS WATER
1 CUP PINEAPPLE, DICED
1 CUP MANGO, PEELED AND PITTED

1 TEASPOON LEMON
1 TEASPOON SPIRULINA
2 TEASPOONS WHEAT GRASS POWDER

Mix spinach and the water. Peel the pineapple and mango and cut into chunks. Add remaining ingredients and blend again.

EVENING GLORY

In the jungle of the night, a green smoothie can increase your strength and make you glow against the dark sky.

2 CUPS SPINACH
2 CUPS WATER
1 PEAR, CORED
½ CUCUMBER, PEELED
½ LIME, JUICED
½ AVOCADO, PEELED AND PITTED

Mix the spinach with water. Add chunks of pears and cucumber as well as lime juice. Blend again. Mix in the scooped-out avocado. Add water until desired consistency is reached.

PEAR DELICIOUS

2 PEARS, CORED
1 AVOCADO, PEELED AND PITTED
1 HANDFUL OF LAMB'S LETTUCE
1 HANDFUL OF CORIANDER OR CILANTRO
1 CUP WATER
1 TSP OF MACA POWER (OPTIONAL)
A LITTLE HONEY IF EXTRA SWEETNESS IS
    NEEDED

Blend all ingredients with ice until smooth. Taste,
and if your pears were not the really sweet kind,
add a little honey.

APPLE CREAM

Popeye would approve of this flavorful combination of apple, avocado, and spinach, as it is also a power booster with the
added help of spirulina, which contains higher protein levels than red meat. This creamy concoction packs a healthy punch
of flavor!

2 HANDFULS ORGANIC SPINACH
1 ORGANIC APPLE, PEELED AND CORED
½ AVOCADO, PEELED AND PITTED
2 TEASPOON SPIRULINA
½ LEMON, JUICED
½ CUP COCONUT MILK
1 CUP WATER
1–2 CUPS ICE

Place all ingredients in your NutriBullet and blend.
If needed, juice apple first or cut into smaller pieces.
Blend until creamy and smooth. Serve with a straw.

HONEY BUNCH

1–2 CUPS HONEYDEW, DICED
¼ AVOCADO, PEELED AND PITTED
1 LARGE HANDFUL SPINACH
1 MEDIUM CUCUMBER, PEELED

Blend with water and ice to desired consistency.

COSMO CHILLER

1–2 CUPS MUSTARD GREENS
1 MEDIUM CUCUMBER, PEELED
1 CUP FROZEN CRANBERRIES
1 LIME, PEELED
½ LEMON, PEELED
3–5 MINT LEAVES

Blend with water and ice to desired consistency.

SALSA FRESCA

1 CUP CILANTRO
1 CUP PARSLEY
½ LEMON, PEELED
1 APPLE, CORED
GINGER TO TASTE
1–2 STALKS CELERY

Blend with water to desired consistency.

HEAVY GREEN

Green-drink newbies need not apply; this one is for the hard-core green enthusiast. With minimal amounts of fructose, this offering is perfect for those with blood sugar issues. Spinach, broccoli, and collards!

1 CUP BROCCOLI
2 LEAVES COLLARD GREENS
1 CUP SPINACH
½ GREEN APPLE, CORED
½ CUCUMBER, PEELED
½ AVOCADO, PEELED AND PITTED
1 LIME, JUICED

Add all ingredients. Blend until smooth, adding water as necessary.

INDEX

Super Smoothies for Nutribullet

NOTES

_____

_____

_____

_____

_____

_____

_____

_____

_____

_____

_____

_____

_____

_____

_____

_____

_____

_____

_____

_____

_____

_____

_____

_____

Green Smoothie Joy for NutriBullet

By Cressida Elias

Green Smoothie Joy for NutriBullet teaches you how to create an array of delicious and healthy green smoothies using your NutriBullet (the recipes will also work in other blenders). Additionally, this book gives you the tools to invent your own great-tasting green smoothies. The health benefits of these smoothies are tremendous—so start extracting now!

$16.99 Hardcover

ISBN 978-1-63450-700-4

The Complete Healthy Smoothie for NutriBullet

By Jason Manheim

While Manheim's recipes are fantastic on their own, they can also easily be used as templates to expand your Nutribullet smoothie repertoire. Learn about adding healthy fats such as virgin olive oil, avocado, and coconut oil, and get advice on eliminating separation and foam. Everything you need to energize, look good, and feel great with healthy smoothies is packed within.

$16.99 Hardcover

ISBN 978-1-63450-871-1

The Green Smoothie Miracle

By Erica Palmcrantz Aziz

This book has everything you need to know about green smoothies and how you can make these delicious, healthy drinks. Green smoothies are made from leafy greens that give you a boost of chlorophyll (sun energy), minerals and vitamins; they will make you shine like the sun! Learn how this green miracle drink will strengthen your immune system, boost organ health, and promote weight loss at the same time, all while tasting great.

$19.95 Hardcover

ISBN 978-1-62087-061-7

GREEN SMOOTHIES & PROTEIN DRINKS

50 Recipes to Get Fit, Lose Weight, and Look Great

Jason Manheim

Green Smoothies & Protein Drinks

By Jason Manheim

The green smoothie is hands down the best supplement to any diet. With at least one green smoothie a day, your body will not only receive an extra boost of nutrients, but will eventually crave these healthier foods naturally. Slowly but surely, unhealthy foods will be replaced by healthier counterparts, and your overall diet and well-being will benefit from the change.

$16.95 Hardcover

ISBN 978-1-62087-601-5

SUPERFOOD
JUICES, SMOOTHIES & DRINKS

Advice and Recipes to Lose Weight, Prevent Illness, and
Improve Your Emotional and Physical Health

JASON MANHEIM

AUTHOR OF
THE HEALTHY
GREEN DRINK
DIET

Superfood Juices, Smoothies & Drinks

By Jason Manheim

Superfoods include apples, bananas, avocados, cherries, chia seeds, dark chocolate, carrots, green tea, hot peppers, kiwis, mangoes, nuts and oats, lemons and limes, peaches, spinach, Swiss chard, and many more foods that you can easily grab at your neighborhood grocery store.

$16.95 Hardcover

ISBN 978-1-62914-592-1

The Healthy Green Drink Diet

By Jason Manheim

A cleansing detox drink is a fantastic, tasty way to consume all your necessary vitamins and minerals without having to resort to a processed multivitamin. Plus, green-drinkers quickly start to crave more fruits and vegetables, leading them to a healthier diet over all. *The Healthy Green Drink Diet* gives health enthusiasts all the tools they need to add green drinks to their daily routine and feel the wonderful, energizing results through and through.

$16.95 Hardcover

ISBN 978-1-61608-473-8

DANIELLA CHACE, MSc, CN

HEALING SMOOTHIES

100 RESEARCH-BASED, DELICIOUS RECIPES *that* PROVIDE NUTRITION SUPPORT *for* CANCER PREVENTION *and* RECOVERY

Healing Smoothies

By Daniella Chace

The ingredients section of the book provides more than sixty cancer-healing foods that are perfect smoothie additions. Cancer patients and their care providers can use these smoothie recipes or create their own from the ingredients list to help heal and nourish the patient throughout the treatment process. In addition, many of the nutrients in these smoothies have been found to support remission and reduce the risk for cancer recurrence.

$16.99 Hardcover

ISBN 978-1-63220-447-9

Detox 101

By Jessi Andricks

Detox 101 is your twenty-one-day guide to cleansing without deprivation. In this program, you will clean out your body, mind, and soul to bring you back to a whole, healthy, and happy you for life. You'll be guided through twenty-one days of healthy eating, drinking, moving, and thinking. You'll learn simple ways to incorporate healthy habits into your daily life as well as do some deep cleansing for all your systems.

$17.95 Hardcover

ISBN 978-1-62914-717-8

For the Love of Food and Yoga

By Liz Price-Kellogg and Kristen Taylor

Written by a yoga student and teacher, *For The Love Of Food And Yoga: A Celebration Of Mindful Eating And Being* is a visually rich exploration of how the inner awareness we develop on our yoga mats fuels our bodies, minds and overall states of well-being, which subsequently impacts our lifestyles and food experiences. This book is comprised of 100 "YogiBites"—a collection of time-tested yoga teachings—paired with 100 original, soul-satiating recipes that are vegetarian, vegan, or raw.

$24.99 Hardcover

ISBN 978-1-63450-351-8

THE GREEN AISLE'S
HEALTHY SMOOTHIES
AND SLUSHIES

More Than 75 Healthy Recipes to
Help You Lose Weight and Get Fit

MICHELLE SAVAGE

The Green Aisle's Healthy Smoothies and Slushies

By Michelle Savage

Chocolate cheesecake, mango tango, and cinnamon toast. Broccoli boost, zucchini nut bread, and sweet and spicy apple. These are just a few of the energizing and nutritious drink recipes you can find in Michelle Savage's *The Green Aisle's Healthy Smoothies and Slushies*. This book is full of beverages that are tasty, healthy, and easy to make—all you need is a blender. All featured ingredients are easily found in grocery stores, at farmers' markets, or in specialty food stores—and some are even available on Savage's blog and website, BrowseTheGreenAisle.com.

$16.95 Hardcover

ISBN 978-1-62914-575-4